CHRISTIAN YOUTH

It's Cool to Believe in God for

Love, Acceptance, Friendship, Protection, and Direction

ROBERT MOMENT

LEGAL STATEMENT

Christian Youth © 2013 by Robert Moment.
All rights reserved.

ISBN-13: 978-0-9799982-9-4

LIABILITY/WARRANTY

Table of Contents

Introduction - The God Who Knows Your Future

Let us pray:
The God Who Knows Your Future

Dear Heavenly Father,
Thank You for accepting and loving me
unconditionally. My future is in Your hands.
I celebrate Your love, faithfulness,
goodness and truth.
I need Your love... Your guidance... Your power...
Your wisdom... and Your protection,
each and every day.
Thank You for Your presence and peace.
I trust You with my life.
In Jesus' name, Amen.

God knows **your name**. God **sees** your **incredible value**. The Scriptures say, "My future is in Your hands." (Psalms 30 1:15) Nothing can be more true today, for people of all ages. However, this knowledge is especially important for young people to remember.

God loves YOU! Each and every one of us is precious in God's eyes. He tells us so in the Bible, encouraging us to aspire to greater things, purer spirits, and devotion to Him. What happens if we haven't done all these things? He *still* loves you!

Let your Heavenly Father be the most important person in your life.

"See how very much our Heavenly Father loves us."
(1 John 3:1)

Sure, we all get wrapped up in day to day life, dealing with friends, rules, problems, and decisions, but overall, we should always remember that there's someone greater than us always ready to provide support, lend a helping hand, and offering a shoulder to lean on in times of trouble.

What God Has to Offer YOU

We don't have to be perfect in order to accept God's love. God will always love you and always has your best interests in mind. After all, we're only human, with the failings of humans. We make mistakes. We make poor decisions. Sometimes, we do stupid things, because we're only thinking about ourselves, we want to be accepted by our peers, or we're just plain rebellious as we try to 'find' ourselves.

When you look in the mirror, what do you see? Do you see a child, a teenager, or a young adult? How do you perceive yourself? Looking at your own reflection in the mirror, what do you think God has in store for you? Look down at your hands and ask yourself, "What does God want me to do with these?"

God works in mysterious ways. We grow up learning that God often leads us down paths we didn't expect. We face troubles, pain and obstacles and we sometimes wonder why. However, it's important for Christian youth to accept and rise to the challenge offered by such obstacles, as each of them provides us an opportunity to learn, improve, and aspire to greater things.

Unlike many of your peers and friends at school, God loves you, no matter what you look like. For God, it's what's on the inside that counts. God will always love you regardless of what you look like.

As a youth, you wonder how to achieve success in life. Here's a formula for success - always put God first in your life – every day. Put God first and your efforts will be recognized. We love our siblings, our parents, our grandparents, and our friends, but we should love God even more. God loves unconditionally. God loves you, without expecting you to be perfect. God loves you without a bunch of strings attached. In God's love, we enjoy a love that we can always trust.

Many of us have heard the words, "I don't love you anymore," from a girlfriend, boyfriend, or even a fiancé or spouse. Those words are some of the most painful that anyone could ever hear, but take comfort in the fact that God's love is not only unconditional, but also everlasting. As it says in (Romans 5:8) God loves you and wants a relationship with you.

What, exactly does God offer? He offers acceptance, friendship, protection, and a sense of direction. We'll explore these topics in greater detail throughout this book, but for now, realize that acceptance means just that. No matter your gender, your age, your race, or your weight, God accepts you and loves you. No one else could ever love you or understand you like God does.

When it comes to friendship, you have a best friend who will never leave you. With God, you are never alone. Friends come and go, but God is there, yesterday, today, tomorrow, and forever. God will never abandon you. How many friends can you say that about? How many friends can you guarantee will never move away, never grow angry and leave you, or get married and start a family, leaving you behind? God will never do that. God says that He will never leave us nor forsake us. How cool is that?

When it comes to protection, no one offers it better than God. God is always with you, always protecting you even when you don't think you need it. The book of Psalms says, "*I will protect those who know My name.*" (Psalm 90 1:14)

How many of you are unsure about your destiny? How many of you always know exactly which direction to take, which decision to make, or where you're supposed to go today, tomorrow, or ten years from now? God provides direction and guidance.

God loves for us to ask Him questions when we need to make decisions. Why does He like us to ask so many questions? Because He has all the answers! There are many ways that we question decisions: what do you say when you don't know what to do in a certain situation and you need help? You're likely to come up with two different scenarios:

- "Oh, God, what am I going to do?"

- "God help me, what are you going to do?"

Which do you ask? The correct answer is the second one. It's God who has unlimited resources and power. Place your doubts, questions and uncertainties in God's hands, and He will take care of them for you. If you chose the first answer, you limit yourself to your own power and resources, which is no match for God's.

Always ask God what you're going to do about something, or how He is going to help you. Relinquish your paltry sense of power and control. Let go and let God do it. Ask God for instructions, direction, or guidance because He knows the way. God provides His own GPS (we call it God's positioning system) which is critical in today's uncertain environments.

Asking God for direction and guidance helps keep us on the right and true path. Asking God's guidance and direction helps prevent us from becoming lost. When we don't rely on God and ask Him questions, we often end up in situations, relationships, and places that aren't the best for us. God will never lead you down the wrong path.

"I will instruct you and teach you in the way you should go." (Psalm 32:8)

As you read through this book, do your best to stay on track. God can motivate and inspire if you keep Him first in your life. Make every decision based on the will of God, because with God by your side, you can face anything in life. Whatever challenges, difficulties or uncertainties you go through in life, remember the affirmation, "God is my help."

"My help comes from the Lord, who made the heavens and the earth!" (Psalm 121:2)

Let us pray:
God is My Help

Thank You for being with me right now.
Thank You for loving me.
In every situation or problem that I face,
I'm going to seek Your guidance and Your answers.
I give this situation or problem (fill in the blank
with your situation or problem) over to You.
I place my hope and complete trust in You.
In Jesus' name, Amen.

The scriptures offer guidance for all of us in our times of need. Take these three verses, for example:

"Trust in the Lord with all your heart."
(Proverbs 3:5)

"Have faith in God." (Mark 11:22)
"For nothing will be impossible with God."
(Luke 1:37)

Always remember that YOU are God's masterpiece. God created you in His own image. (Ephesians 2:10)

Never give up in your life. Yes, we all face stumbling blocks, but it's what we do with those stumbling blocks that matters to God. Your life matters to God, and God will never give up on you. If God never gives up on you, why would you give up on yourself? Yes, today it may seem dark, dreary and frightening, but tomorrow offers a new beginning. With every new day, we gain strength, purpose, and determination. In times of weakness, turn to God. He is there for you! Always!

You don't have to speak fancy words to pray and commune with God. Keep it simple and speak from your heart. Praying is just another way of conversing with God. Be honest with God, because He knows your innermost thoughts better than you do. Keep in mind that we all make mistakes, regardless of age. God uses our mistakes to teach us, to correct us, to instruct us, protect us, direct us, and perfect us.

As you read through this book, keep your Bible close to hand. Read the passages we mention to give you comfort and strength. God is with you, and will open your heart, and your eyes to a more fulfilling life. Listen to what your Heavenly Father says about you. Receive your value from your Heavenly Father. Doing so will help you feel accepted, approved, loved, secure, confident, and forgiven. In God's eyes, you are a winner. So look in the mirror again and see a winner.

Don't grumble about your problems when talking to God, but talk about your problems in relation to how big God is, and how God can help direct us through our problems, issues, or decisions. When facing such obstacles, it's important to choose your faith over your fear. Recall the 23rd Psalm, which says, "Yea, though I walk through the valley of the shadow of death, I will fear no evil, for Thou art with me, Thy rod and Thy staff, they comfort me."

God is with us, even in our most fearful moments. God is there when we face small problems as well as large ones. He's there when we face despair, grief, and terror. He's there when we experience joy, pleasure, and laughter. Remember that God accepts us no matter what we look like. He loves us, even though we're not perfect. He approves of us when we strive to improve ourselves, and He increases our confidence and sense of security. Best of all, God forgives us of our sins. Large or small, rest assured your sins will be forgiven if you just ask.

As children, teenagers and young adults, it's often hard to curb our tongue. Even as adults, we often have difficulty watching what we say or how we say it. Remember that the words you speak throughout your life can have a huge impact on not only yourself, but also your friends, family, and even strangers. Most of all, the words you speak can have a large impact on God. Strive to speak in a positive manner that blesses you, your life, and the lives of others.

Remember to always choose your faith over fear, and you can become everything that God created you to be. Don't be afraid or hesitant to create a fresh, new vision and direction for your life. Every day is a gift from God, and God has solutions to every problem you will ever face in life. God knows what you will need not only today, but tomorrow, next week, next month, and even five years from now.

Your life is in God's hands. Your future is in God's hands. God has amazing things planned for your future. Not every step of the way will be a picnic. Sometimes, we are tested and challenged in our faith, but rest assured that He will be with you, every step of the way.

Take every challenge, obstacle or disappointment you face in life and learn something from it. Use those lessons to improve yourself, to increase your faith and your devotion to God. Even when we're disappointed, it's for a reason. In the book of Romans, God says that all things work together for the good of those who love God (Romans 8:28).

That is very true. Sometimes, we're surprised to find ourselves where we are, without really understanding how we got onto this path, or how we ended up in a certain situation or even destination. We all make plans in life, much like people make travel plans. However, God's roadmap is not the same as ours. God may have us taking the scenic route when we expected to drive the freeway, or vice versa. The important thing is to trust in God, for He will guide you in the direction you should go. When you have God as your compass, you will never be lost, no matter where you find yourself in life.

Don't be afraid to pray with boldness. Create bold prayers, as we serve a big God. Listen to God. Listen with your heart. Be careful who you listen to. Sometimes, your friends, family or acquaintances don't know what's best for you, but God always does. Resist temptation and allow God to guide you through life. When God is in your heart, you will know the way you should go.

Chapter 1: You are God's Masterpiece

Each day, and say these words:

God loves me;
God is guiding me
God is protecting me
God is showing me how to live my life.

Remember that you are God's masterpiece. There is only one of you, and you are unique and special. Every human being has the potential to offer something unique and special to their family, their friends, acquaintances, or to the world. Remember that God loves you unconditionally and is always present in your life.

How does God mold each and everyone of us? Remember that God sees us as His precious gifts. We are His priceless treasures from His kingdom. How can He see us this way, despite our faults, sins, and behaviors? Because we are created in His image, and nothing is more precious or special than to be created in God's own image. God is the Lord of all creation, and *He made you for a reason*.

It's always important to remember and remind yourself that God is continually shaping your life based on His character. While we often fail along the way, God desires us to become more like Him in every way and in every aspect of our lives. We are clay and God is the potter, shaping and forming us to His own purposes, enabling us to become the vessels that He then fills with His Holy Spirit.

Also keep in mind that this process is ongoing, and we never stop learning, growing, or improving ourselves. However, we can only do this if we submit to God and surrender our will to our Heavenly Father.

We must take comfort and security in the fact that He will shape us according to His will, and on His own timetable.

Many of us, especially at a young age, wonder what we're destined for. Many of us are dissatisfied with our present life or existence, and don't know how we can improve ourselves for the future. Try not to be discouraged, because God is with you.

Even in the most dire of circumstances, be grateful that you are not alone.

Today, many youth don't want to admit to friends that they believe in God, or a higher power, but don't be embarrassed or ashamed to claim your faith. With faith comes confidence, and with confidence comes hope. Every step you take closer to God allows you to take a greater pleasure on your walk with God, knowing that God has something in mind for you. That something might happen tomorrow, next year, or ten years from now. Be patient.

God will guide us in the way we are to go, and He'll take you where you need to be, and where He wants you to be. Just remember that God is always working on you, from the inside out. Take comfort from the fact and solace that you receive, knowing that you can love God, and He loves you unconditionally. If you allow God to enter your heart, He will continue to make you better, in strength, in spirit, and perseverance. Yes, God loves you just the way you are right now, but He can also continually strive to improve and change your heart to go in the way He leads.

"The Lord said to him, 'Who gave man his mouth? Who makes him deaf or mute? Who gives sight or makes him blind? Is it not I, the Lord? Now go; I will help you speak and will teach you what to say."
(Exodus 4:11-12)

How does God create you into His masterpiece? How do we recognize His touch as He takes our unfinished molds of clay and creates us into a beautiful and complete vessel for His Holy Spirit? Simply, remember that God works on molding us every day. Every contact you have with a friend, a family member, or a stranger impacts your life in some way. Every day, you learn lessons. You see God's mercy and love, or you find new strength through determination, resolve, or humility.

There is not one single relationship in your life that isn't part of God's making in some way. As much as you leave an impact on everyone you meet, so do people who touch your life. They leave a mark on the pottery of your own soul. Strive for greater peace, security and comfort in your life, regardless of your circumstances.

If you want a closer relationship with God, help Him in His desire to create a new or worthy vessel. Stop hanging around the negative people in life that do nothing but drag you down. Associate with those who follow God and God's way, for they also help God shape you through their example of Christian love.

We also become God's masterpiece by our actions. The more we listen to God and live as a Christian, following the guidelines, lessons and words of Jesus, and allow the Holy Spirit to guide us, the more God guides our steps along the right path. It's a natural progression. The more you do in life that is compassionate, right, and good, the greater your desire to continue doing these things.

You can always look to God for support, and He'll be there to give it. Let God enter your heart and shape your heart's desire to guide you along the path so that eventually, you can meet His goals and hopes for you.

Remember that God created you. You are His masterpiece. He knows everything about you and will guide you.

"I praise you because I am fearfully and wonderfully made; your works are wonderful, I know that full well. My frame was not hidden from you
when I was made in the secret place. When I was woven together in the depths of the earth, your eyes saw my unformed body. All the days ordained for me were written in your book before one of them came to be."
(Psalm 130 9:14-16)

Chapter 2: God has a Plan for Your Life

It may not seem like it all the time, but God is thinking of you. He knows about your worries, your concerns, and your plans for the future. He knows that many of us are uncertain about what that future holds, but His teachings always strive to encourage us to rely on His guidance when it comes to making decisions.

No matter what you're going through, it's important for Christian youth to understand that God is a loving and merciful God. The things that you're going through right now may seem so important, so stressful, and so frustrating, but God is bigger than all those problems.

God understands everything about you, and what you're going through. He knows how you feel and what's going on in your head. The best thing about that is that God believes in you. He believes that you have the capability of fulfilling all of the things that He has destined for you to fulfill.

"For I know the plans I have for you," says the Lord. They are plans for good and not for disaster, to give you a future and a hope." (Jeremiah 29:11)

With God's strength, you *can* overcome obstacles in your life. Many of the obstacles we face on a daily basis are created in our own world - by sin, sinful living, temptation, greed, or jealousy. We are all sinners, but we all have the opportunity to learn from our sins, as well as to be forgiven for them. Jesus' sacrifice gave that fellowship back to each and every one of us, along with the ability make that choice. God has given us a choice. He hopes you'll make the right one.

God has a plan for every single one of us, to live in victory. His belief that you will embrace your destiny, and follow it, is certain.

"The Lord will guide you continually."
(Isaiah 58:11)

It's All About Trust

As a young adult (although this goes for any age), it's important for us as Christians to trust in God. Without trust, there is no faith. Where there is no faith, there is no direction. You are a Christian youth. What does that mean? It means that you have made a choice to live for God, according to the instructions and guidelines offered in the Bible.

You may not always achieve the things you strive to do, or things that you see other young people do, but that doesn't mean that you have failed to please God. God understands your feeling and has given you the grace to be able to live for Him.

The Bible says that nothing, nothing at all, can separate you from God's love, and no matter where you've been, or what you have done, God will accept you with open arms. He wants to be your best friend. His love is unconditional, and He will always love you, no matter how many times you fail.

Right now, this very minute, tell God that you love Him, and ask Him to help you live for Him. Mean it from the depth of your heart. Give yourself up to the Lord, and He will guide your path. You may think that your friends, your parents, or your teachers just don't understand you, but God does. He understands every little thing about you, including your flaws, your faults, and your strengths. God also gives us strength to withstand and overcome every temptation placed in our path.

Temptation comes in many shapes, sizes and forms. Temptation is often disguised, but it leads us to do things that we know we shouldn't. Have you ever been tempted to steal? Have you been tempted to cheat? Have you been tempted to lie? Most of us have. Temptations face us every day. Sometimes, we succeed and overcome, and sometimes we don't. Regardless, and no matter what you do, God will always understand and love you.

How could He not, when He made you? The Bible says that God formed you when you were in the womb, and that He knew you, even then. No one else, not even your parents, a grandparent, a cousin,or a friend, can understand you or love you more than God. Revel in that love. Take comfort in the understanding that you can find in God.

Be encouraged by that support and walk in the promises that God has provided for you. Remember that no matter what obstacles you may face now, next week, next month or next year, God believes in your ability to overcome. He loves you!

"Remember, I am with you always, to the end of the age." (Matthew 28:20)

"Blessed are those who trust in the Lord, whose trust is the Lord." (Jeremiah 17:7)

Knowing Where You're Going

All of us have made short-term and long-term plans, whether it's regarding school, what we'll do over summer vacation, or what we'd like to do after we graduate. Sometimes those plans work out and sometimes they don't.

It's important for Christian youth to believe and look to God for direction in their lives. Who are you? Where are you going? Every one of us has asked that question, and often, we don't believe we've received an answer. However, when you believe and trust in God, the answers are always within reach.

We may be pulled in many directions; our teachers, our parents, and our friends strive to guide us, or tempt us, to do what *they* think should be done. Even when your own mind struggles with making decisions, sticking to plans, or providing you with a sense of direction, you're often confused and uncertain. Ultimately, when it comes right down to it, God is the only compass you need. When you want to know which way to go, or which decision is right for you, ask God.

Remember, you were made by Him. You were made to look the way you do because you are God's creation. You are a child of God, and, because He made you, He loves you the way you are. Don't be discouraged if you don't feel you're pretty enough, handsome enough, or smart enough to do what you want to do in life.

Don't listen to other people when they tell you that you're dumb, you're ugly, or you're too fat, or any other disparaging and bullying remarks. Remember that God made you, and your presence states that He thinks otherwise. Believe in Him. It's His opinion that counts, not those who resort to bullying or sarcastic criticism.

When you follow God, you'll always go in the right direction. Sometimes, that direction or path you take may not be easy. In fact, sometimes taking the right path is the hardest thing you'll ever do. On occasion, even friends and family members may be confused or disappointed in your choices. Sometimes, you'll be able to explain to them why you made certain decisions, and they may understand. Sometimes, they won't. Their disappointment, remarks, and opinions are not as important as your trust in fellowship with God. God will guide you in the direction you will go, and it's important to be confident in God's choices and decisions for you.

Many of us, especially in our youth, are tempted and distracted by worldly things. We allow ourselves to be led astray, to hang out with people who have a bad influence on us, who encourage us to do things we know we shouldn't. If your heart is open to God, He can redirect your path. This is not saying that you don't share the blame or the responsibility for your sins, or when you do something bad, because God does give us a final choice in every one of our actions.

However, if we repent, sincerely apologize, and make honest efforts to come back to God, to follow His guidelines and His teachings, He will be there to guide you. He will be there to support you, and to give you strength when temptation rears its ugly head again.

That's one of the most wonderful things about God. He truly has the ability and the desire to forgive - and forget - our sins, and loves us always.

God I Am Available for You

The title above is a phrase that warms God's heart every time He hears it. In fact, the greatest gift we can give to the Lord is our service to Him.

"Commit to the Lord whatever you do, and your plans will succeed." (Proverbs 16:3)

The key to truly being available to God is having a heart of surrender and sacrifice. Be bold! Don't stop there! After you tell the Lord you are available, ask Him what He wants you to do! Open up your heart to the many possibilities to serve Him that are available in this world.

Submitting to God's will is the ultimate sacrifice to the Lord, and one that can foster change in others. Remember that when we don't make ourselves available to God, it is harder for Him to touch our spirits.

What if God were unavailable to us as we sometimes are to Him? It can be difficult to take on the mantle of sacrifice and allow God's plan for us to take shape. Sometimes God takes us into uncomfortable places where our beliefs may be questioned or where others may spurn our attempts to reach out to them.

But think about God's experience with humankind. How often have we turned our back on God, ignored His wisdom and even shut out His love?

We must make ourselves fully available to God, just as He is always fully available to us.

There is an old saying that, "Life is not a spectator sport." Neither is being a Christian! We must live the lives God has planned for us, and the only way to do that is to jump in with both feet and *live* God's word, not simply study it.

So today, pray not only for God's plan for your life, but to let Him know that you are here for Him, just as He is here for you. Honestly, lay down your own agenda and become open to what God desires of you.

When we take that step to say, "Here I am! Send me!" We'll soon discover that the rewards for being completely available to God are infinite and far greater than what we could have imagined for ourselves.

Conclusion

Don't worry about what other people may think. Especially in our teenage years, peer pressure, opinions and sarcasm can have a big impact on our emotional and mental well-being and sense of security. However, never be ashamed of believing in God.

Never be embarrassed to stand up for God and Jesus. It's not stupid or hokey to live your life this way. He's the only one that is always there, every minute, in times of joy and in times of despair. Friends come and go. Most friends aren't loyal to the core, but God is.

God teaches us and guides us to a better way to live our lives with faith, love, and grace. Without God in our lives, we face no sure future. Without God, you're at the mercy of a world that doesn't always have your best interests at heart.

God is constant. God is the same today as He was yesterday. God will be the same tomorrow as He was today. Take faith and security in that. God will never stop loving you. ***God will use you right where you are today !***

Chapter 3: God's Love for You

Many of us experience uncertainty, doubt, and questions as we grow, but one thing that is **always** constant is God's love for you. Only God can fulfill many of our needs, five of which include love, acceptance, security, identity, and purpose. These are human needs that are emotional in nature rather than physical. After all, if we have shelter, food and water, we can survive. However, our spirit also needs our emotional needs to be fulfilled in order to survive - and thrive.

We often seek to find these things in ourselves or through others; they're often difficult, if not impossible, to expect from our friends, our family, or our future spouses. That's not because they're not trying, it's because they're human. So are we. God is so much greater than that, and has the capability and capacity to provide fulfillment of all our physical and emotional needs.

Remember what we said about God's love being ever present and unconditional? If you've ever had a best friend, or someone you loved very much that you felt you could trust, you have an inkling of what it might be like to rely on someone totally, completely, and without fear or worry. However, even the best human relationships can end. Friends move away, loved ones die, and situations and circumstances can often destroy our faith in others.

Many of us are incapable of completely trusting or relying on someone else for our emotional or physical well-being. This doesn't happen when you have a relationship with God. Because God loves you unconditionally, He never changes and never ends. Nothing in this world, and nothing you can do, will change His love for you. Be assured that God will never leave or forsake you. You will always and forever find security and comfort through this special relationship with God, because this relationship, like God himself, is eternal.

You don't have to be perfect. We've said it before, and we'll say it again. More human. We will make mistakes. We will stray. The thing is, no matter how many mistakes you make, no matter what you look like, or no matter what you do, you won't let God down. God loves you unconditionally.

He loves you without measure, and He doesn't have any hidden agenda, reservations, or stipulations for that love. God guides you through every aspect and experience in your life. This guidance is not something you earn, but is a gift from God because He loves you, unconditionally.

In times of doubt, stress, troubles, despair, or grief, God will be there for you. When your friends scatter, God will be there. When it seems as if nothing but dark clouds surround you, God's light will shine through them and show you the way. God's guiding light is unconditional love.

Check out these following verses that exemplify that love:

"I trust in God's unfailing love forever and ever."
(Psalm 52:8)

"For great is your steadfast love toward me."
(Psalm 86:13)

"I am with you always, to the end of the age."
(Matthew 28:20)

God is your best friend, this is comfort to us when we're troubled, to give us support and encouragement when we struggle with obstacles or challenges, and most of all, to love us, every second, every hour of every day. God is **always** there for us to turn to when things get tough, especially when we don't think anyone else will understand where we're coming from.

God is the only one that you can be sure of in any situation, good or bad. God always puts you first, and His friendship is eternal. If you haven't experienced that deep, abiding closeness and friendship with the Lord, you are missing out on one of the most exciting, rewarding, and satisfying friendships you will ever have.

Unlike our earthly friends, God never expects anything in return. All He wants is our love. He doesn't need your help, won't ask for favors, and doesn't need you to prove anything to Him. All He asks is that we love Him. In return, He is always there for us. No other friendship in our human realm of experience can compare to that kind of a friendship.

We make friends through our lives, but as we grow up, we often drift apart. We move away, we get married, or get new jobs. As we age, our interests and circumstances also change. Sometimes, friendships end because of something said, a disagreement, or a sense of betrayal.

While this is common in human relationships, God doesn't change, regardless of our circumstances. He stands as our friend and guide, whether we're young or old, rich or poor, single or married. He gives us as many chances as we need to overcome our difficulties. If we make a mistake, He's right there to forgive us. He continues to love us and remain steadfastly by our side, always prepared to protect, shelter and lift us up as long as we are willing to let Him do so.

"Draw close to God,
and God will draw close to you." (James 4:8)

Isn't it reassuring to know that you have a friend forever, a friend who will remain loyal and steadfast every day of your life? God is there **all the time**. Even when we stray from Him, or get so caught up in our daily lives that we fail to daily commune with Him, He will be there when we return. As long as you return to God, ask for His guidance, you can remain secure in the knowledge that He will be there for you.

With God, you don't have to ask yourself if you made one too many mistakes. You don't have to ask how many times you can be forgiven. God doesn't keep score.

"He offers his friendship to the godly."
(Proverbs 3:32)

God doesn't put any restrictions on what He expects from people. If you are Godly, He offers His friendship to you. You don't have to be perfect. You don't have to go to church every Sunday, to pay certain tithes, or worry about making occasional mistakes.

All God asks of us is that we love Him, and strive to be the best we can be, following His words when it comes to how we live our lives. God doesn't put any restrictions or boundaries on how or when He offers His friendship.

So, who is your best friend? Make God your best friend today, and you'll soon understand that He is truly the only one you can count on every day, in every aspect of your life, not only today, next month, or next year, but until the end of time.

Remember that God will never give up on you. He provides each and every one of us, no matter where we come from, how old or young we are, or what we look like, the gifts to love and forgive not only ourselves, but also others. These spiritual gifts may grace us all, if we choose to accept them.

Unfortunately, many of us are unwilling to use those gifts due to our own unwillingness or inability to forgive others. Yes, it's part of human nature to give up on ourselves, most often because others have given up on us. Either that, or we worry about failing or having someone think we've failed, in the future.

How many times do you think you would have the patience to forgive someone for something they did? Many of us don't have the patience to forgive endlessly and love someone despite their many faults and sins. Many of us have been let down by someone we relied on. Sometimes, a friend or a family member has lied to us so many times that we can't believe them anymore. A friend, a girlfriend or boyfriend, or even a parent or spouse has sworn up and down that he or she would change, but because they failed to realize their promises so many times before, we don't think it's possible.

Our ability to believe in others is slowly destroyed when we've been let down by others. God is different. He doesn't expect us to prove ourselves to Him. No matter how many times we fail, or fall short, He's there to forgive us. He's there waiting to love us, offering comfort and strength. Take comfort in the fact that you never have to go through anything alone, for God's presence and His love is our constant companion. That presence and love doesn't rely or depend on anything we do. We cannot **prove** ourselves good enough or trustworthy enough for God.

In God's eyes, we are always loved.

"The Lord protects the simple; when I was brought low, he saved me." (Psalm 116:6)

God's love is not based on what we do or don't do. God's love is a gift, one of the greatest in the universe. His love is unconditional. What does that mean? It means that no matter how many times you let Him down, or break a promise, or lie, He never gives up on you. This knowledge should give each and every one of us strength and confidence to improve, to overcome, and to live a more godly life.

Take this time to remember Christ's last words to His disciples. His disciples were simple, hard-working men who made many mistakes in their lives when trying to follow in His footsteps. When He appeared to them after the crucifixion, He reminded them that they had much to do - in God's name.

They were scared, confused, and filled with doubt about their own abilities to do so. Jesus wasn't disappointed in them, and He didn't turn His back on them. Instead, before ascending to His father in Heaven, Christ reminded them that the most important thing to keep in mind was to remain strong in their faith.

*"Remember, I am with you always,
to the end of the age."* (Matthew 28:20)

Approval Seeking

As toddlers, we seek to please our parents so that they smile, hug, accept and love us. We crave their praise. We crave their smiles and their affection. This sense of acceptance elicits feelings of security and stability. As grade school children and heading into our teenage years, we want to be liked by everyone. We want to belong to the "in" or popular crowd or clique at school. Our teenage years are some of the toughest that we'll ever go through. We are judged by our looks, our clothes, our attitude, and our personalities.

As we enter the workforce, we want to be accepted, liked, and appreciated by our co-workers and our boss. We want to be recognized for our ideas, our timeliness, our loyalty and our productivity. We want recognition that shows that we are appreciated, that we are valuable members of a workforce, a project team, or even as individuals, and team leaders, not only in order to gain the benefits of promotion, but for the recognition, self-confidence, and self-esteem that such recognition brings.

We enter into relationships because we seek companionship and love of others. We want that other person in our lives. That person who didn't grow up with us, and probably doesn't work with us, but eventually, they to get to know us, understand us, and appreciated us.

The difficulty with any of these relationships is in the potential of failure. Whether we're school children, teenagers, or in the workforce, things change. Our parents may eventually become disappointed in our actions or decisions. Our school friends move away, go to different schools, or find jobs that eventually fracture groups into a myriad of directions. In the workforce, we lose a job, move to a different department, or relocate, leaving us feeling as if we have to start all over again in our strive for recognition and acceptance.

However, the only true constant in our lives is the unconditional acceptance offered by God. He loves us, no matter what. We said that before, and for good reason. It's true. You don't have to walk a fine line, walk on egg shells, or do everything perfectly in order to obtain God's attention, recognition, or acceptance.

"To the praise of the glory of his grace, wherein He hath made us accepted in the beloved."
(Ephesians 1:6)

You see, you don't have to prove anything to God. He is the one who made you, so He knows who you are. He knows what you can do. He alone knows your true and full potential. Try as hard as we may, we humans are often completely incapable of offering anyone, no matter how much we love them, complete and total acceptance, recognition, and value on a daily basis. We get caught up in our own lives, our own problems, our own desires to be seen, recognized, and accepted.

God's love is steadfast and enduring. This is a difficult concept for humans to understand, but it's one of the most wonderful feelings of joy and security that we can experience.

"All my strength to you I sing praises, for you, oh God, are my refuge, the God who shows me unfailing love." (Psalm 59:17)

Many of us understand that our faith provides us the comfort and strength God offers, but do you really grasp the fact, deep down in your soul of souls, in your heart of hearts, that He loves you unconditionally, and that love is forever unchanging and constant?

As a human, it's difficult for us to grasp the concept of such unreserved love. How can we not feel this way, especially after some of our closest friends, relatives, or love interests have distanced themselves from us, or even let us down?

The only type of love that goes anywhere close to God's unconditional love is the love a parent has for their child. Parents strive to protect their children every day, comfort them when they hurt, and defend them, even when they have disappointed us. Yes, parents get frustrated, impatient, and discouraged, but the power of a mother or father's love is a stronger bond than many people imagine.

Parents don't have to agree with everything their children do, but they love them regardless. God's love for us is similar. With God however, we don't have to live up to specific expectations in order to receive His love. Like a parent, God loves us just the way we are, even with all our weaknesses, faults, and disappointments.

In our personal lives, we always try to be good enough, attractive enough, or interesting enough to receive the recognition and acceptance of others, but with God, that's not necessary. His love is there from the very beginning, and is unfailing, even when we are at our worst.

Remember, God's love doesn't come with strings. He's with us at our best moments, and our worst. God knows everything about you, and has seen and recognized not only your sacrifices, but your sins. If you accept God's love, and open your heart to the goodness that He has prepared for you in the same manner in which it was given (without reservations or conditions) you will find the overwhelming peace and serenity of that unconditional love.

Above all, remember that God will never leave you. He's not a neighborhood friend who moves away. He's not a parent who passes away. He's not a spouse who someday might leave you.

God will never leave you. He's always with you, a concept that is hard for us to understand. God is eternal, and is eternally present in your life. This concept should offer comfort and security in God's abiding presence. Remember that God has been there since the very beginning of your life, and He'll see you through to the end. This is a promise of His love, guidance and protection that no one else in your life can make.

At times, it may seem that God is far away, especially when you're going through difficult times and uncertainties. Sometimes, when we feel

God is furthest from us, He is actually very near. It doesn't matter if you've been too unhappy to pray, or if you've missed a few Sunday services. He still watches over you.

Sometimes, you may feel as if God is avoiding you, but He's not. You are never hidden from His side. Even when your days are troubled, and the sun seems to be hiding behind a thick, black bank of clouds, God is still there, watching over you. He is there. Tonight, you can see the sunset, and tomorrow morning, you will see the sunrise. He is there.

Even when you don't have God close to your heart on a daily basis, He's never far away. You may think God always abides in heaven, among the clouds, but it's important for Christians to understand that God's spirit is within you, each and every day, no matter where you go. A hymn written by Saint Patrick expresses this thought in a wonderful way:

"Christ be with me, Christ within me,
Christ behind me, Christ before me,
Christ beside me, Christ to win me,
Christ to comfort me and restore me,
Christ beneath me, Christ above me."

You see, Saint Patrick understood the concept that God's Spirit inhabits our souls. God's Spirit isn't distant or impersonal, or far away from us. Gain strength from the fact that God's Spirit consistently abides within you and accompanies you wherever you may go.

God accepts you, even when you don't think about Him as you should. Take comfort in the fact that God will never leave you, and that with His Spirit, you have the strength and courage to face any obstacle or any difficulty in life. His acceptance doesn't depend on how good we are, or whether we've gone to church every Sunday, or even if we've done something really bad this past month. God's love for us is unconditional, and He will always be there, always love us, and always be waiting for us to reach out for Him.

God is always there, ready to catch you when you stumble or fall.

Chapter 5: God's Friendship for You

When God is your best friend, you're never alone. After all, earthly friends come and go, but God remains the same today, yesterday, and forever. God will never forget you, move away from you, nor abandon you. How many friends do you have that you can say will never, ever leave you? God says that He will never leave us nor forsake of us. How cool is that?

Our Only True Friend

When we have problems, it's natural to turn to your friends, but our friends don't always give us the answers or the advice that were looking for. Sometimes, their responses to our problems and their solutions from them only lead to more confusion, especially when their ideas or suggestions don't quite match with what we know about ourselves, about our faith, and about God. When you feel like this, it's important to go off somewhere by yourself and talk to God.

God is always with you, and your relationship with Him is a two way street. It's not about God fulfilling every wish you have, like a genie in a bottle, but it's about listening to God. God will tell you what you need to do, and then you meet Him in faith. God knows how all your situations will work out, and the good news is that you're always a part of that solution.

Like friends, God is as close to you as you want Him to be. In getting to know God, recognize His voice and recognize the signs of His presence around you. When you know God, you'll know the feeling of peace, security, and comfort at any time you feel nervous or uncertain. God is always there to help you overcome your anxieties and fears.

The best thing about having God as a friend is that He's always there to listen to you. He will bring peace to your soul. He always leads you to the right solution, as long as you listen. When God offers you a solution, He has your back. He is your sustainer. God won't leave you to handle problems by yourself. However, if you don't listen to God and follow His advice or His solution to your issues, you may risk making your issues or problems worse.

We mentioned just a moment ago that God is the same today, yesterday, and forever. Because of this constancy, we have God as our most powerful weapon against fear and worry. No matter what your problem, fear, or issue, look to the Scriptures for your answers. The Scriptures are there to give us power, reassurance, and security. No matter what your circumstances, you'll find a scripture that pertains to your questions.

Why are the words found in the Scriptures so more powerful than those that anyone else can offer? Because the Word never changes. It remains the same century after century.

The God of today is the God who delivered the Israelites out of bondage. He is the same God that will deliver you today and provide comfort, strength and assurance for your children tomorrow, next year, or 50 years from now. God's love, power and presence are unceasing.

"For I am the Lord, I do not change."
(Malachi 3:6)

Every day, things change. Seasons change, circumstances change. Our lives change. We grow

49

up, we get married, we have children. One day, everything is going great, and the next day we feel as if we've been knocked to our knees. Even those we love, and who love us most, change as time passes.

God, in His ultimate wisdom, understands that we're human and that the human condition requires change. Yes, we experience changes in season and circumstance, but changes also offer predictable patterns. Spring flows into summer, summer to fall, and fall into winter. Spring brings crops and fall brings harvests. Day follows night so that we rest, and when the sun rises in the morning, we wake up feeling refreshed. Even though changes are all around us, there are many changes that provide constancy to our lines. That constancy ensures us that God's love is ever-present in our lives.

Think about nature, and how our universe, our world, and even the animals, plants, and trees found upon the earth were created. They remain the same, as does their growth pattern, giving us reassurance and reliability. Such constancy reminds us that God loves us constantly so we don't have to be afraid. His kindness and loving is eternal and never changes. Even though we change, our jobs change, and our relationships change, God never does. His love is steadfast as He watches over us.

"Give all your worries to God, for He cares what happens to you." (1 Peter 5:7)

Take comfort in the fact that God's friendship is solid, trustworthy, and reliable. When everything in your life seems to be turning upside down or when you feel you have no control over what's happening in your life, at school, with your relationships or your job, turn to God. Let God be your anchor, and you will never be lost. Rely on His friendship, and trust your well-being to His infinite wisdom and mercy.

Chapter 6: God's Protection for You

When you're worried about something, upon whom do you rely? Your friends, your parents, or your teachers? You should rely on all of them, but you should also rely on God.

God provides the ultimate protection. That doesn't mean that bad things don't happen to good people, or that bad things don't happen to people who believe in God. Unfortunately, they do.

When something goes wrong in your life, or if something bad happens to you, who do you blame? Do you blame God? Many people do, but it's often because they don't understand that God's plans for us is different than what many may think they should be. Often, we don't understand God's plans, especially when they involve hurt, pain, fear, or even death. God doesn't want His children to hurt, but when they do, there is a reason. We don't always understand those reasons.

Jesus told His disciples that they would encounter pain and danger for His sake. He knew that they would suffer on His behalf. He knew it would be difficult for them at times, and that they would face challenges, heartache, fear, and even torture and death. However, He also told them that they would meet the blessings of serving Him.

Even when something bad happens to you or a friend, it's important to believe that God has a reason. We are mere mortals, and often fail to understand what those reasons could possibly be. There is that saying that goes, "The wisdom of man is the folly of God."

Even people who have experienced the worst that human life has to offer can rely on God's strength and protection. Use that strength to help others. The testimony, witness and dedication of those who have experienced the worst in life can help guide others to overcome, to reach for salvation, or to increase their faith. The possibilities are limitless. God does care about you. God touches us in many different ways. Do we always understand those ways? No.

However, God can revive us with a sense of security and protection, even when we're facing our greatest challenges. When you imagine yourself cradled in the arms of God, a sense of security comforts and surrounds you. Although our daily circumstances change, God's love for us is eternal.

Sure, we can focus our goals on increasing our bank accounts, or getting those promotions, but promotions and our bank accounts can disappear in the blink of an eye. A person who is at the top of the mountain today may find themselves in the lowest valley tomorrow. It's important for us to remember that no power that we gain for ourselves can protect us from the world's problems.

Money doesn't buy happiness. On the contrary, God provides eternal protection. He is our shelter and security. He will be there to help us weather any storm because He doesn't leave us in times of trouble. God is there to guard our souls and direct our footsteps no matter what happens, if only we ask. Be secure and feel protected within God's abiding and eternal presence and you will always feel safe, even in the worst of times.

Check out this stanza from a song written by Garth Brooks:

"Sometimes I thank God for unanswered prayers
Remember when you're talking to the man upstairs
that just because He doesn't answer doesn't mean
He don't care
Some of God's greatest gifts are
unanswered prayers."

Have you ever wished or prayed for something and then, later on, realized that you were glad it didn't happen? It's important for us to thank God for all the doors that He opens to us, and even more so for the doors that remain closed throughout our lifetime.

After all, God knows what's best for us. We should learn to trust that His wisdom is much greater than ours. God is in perfect control of our destinies, and we may not understand why, or why something is happening, but we need to trust in Him. We don't know what the future has in store for us, and more often than not, we don't want to know.

Be comforted in the fact that God protects you as you move forward in life. He always has your best interest at heart. He's the only one that knows our future and understands that something even better might be just around the corner.

We all face rejection, pain and hurt in our lives. We lose a job, experience a failed relationship, or may not get that promotion we want. Regardless of how many disappointments or rejections we face in life, we must remember to put our faith in God. These temporary rejections are God's way of protecting our future.

Sometimes, He protects us from a future hurt, grief or sorrow by putting us on a certain path right now. Yes, sometimes that path can be difficult and painful to walk, but if we walk in faith and rely on God to comfort and protect us, we will get through that rejection. With each rejection or disappointment in life, we gain strength. We have the potential to emerge victorious, ready to accept the even greater gifts that He has waiting for us in the future.

Disappointments, rejection, and sorrow are not punishments from God! Learn to trust in God, for He is always on your side. Ask for God's will to be done, and not your own. Following God's will provide you the safest place, and one of the most important aspects of faith is trusting that God knows what is right for you, even when we can't or don't understand His reasons.

Keep in mind that when your prayers aren't being answered, it doesn't mean God isn't listening. When your prayers aren't answered, it means that God has something better planned for you that you may find difficult to fathom. He may be protecting you from future sorrow or danger.

Sometimes, the timing isn't right. Regardless, give yourself to Him completely. Earthly rejection is only temporary, but God's plan for you is all encompassing. God's plan will always prevail.

"Trust in the Lord with all your heart and do not rely on your own understanding." (Proverbs 3:5)

"Seek his will in all you do and he will direct your paths." (Proverbs 3:6)

Chapter 7: God's Direction for You

At the introduction of this book, we mentioned that God will give you guidance and give you a direction for leading your life. It's also important to remember that good things, sad things, and bad things do happen to good people. In many aspects, today's youthful generations have grown up faster than any other previous generation, and sometimes, circumstances, incidents and decisions can lead us down the wrong path, especially when you fight against God's will or direction for you.

Listening to God

Most of us don't claim to hear God whispering in our ear, giving us a sense of direction. Sometimes, you may hear someone tell you that they only depend on themselves, because they feel they're the only person they can trust. People think this way because that's what they've experienced in their life. However, there is a better, more sure way to get through life without feeling as if you're alone.

Our parents are supposed to take care of us and provide us with the necessities not only of life, but also in our emotional upbringing. However, due to today's economic pressures and problems, some parents have trouble not only keeping a roof over their head, but food on the table. For many children, the meal they receive at school is the only one they will have all day.

Sometimes, no matter how hard we work, or no matter how hard we try, it's often difficult to take care of not only ourselves, but our loved ones. Don't be ashamed of the fact that your friends may wear new clothes every day, buy lunch at school, or elsewhere, when you're wearing hand-me-downs, clothes from thrift stores, and making do with a peanut butter sandwich. Actually, there's nothing wrong with hand-me-downs or peanut butter sandwiches.

It's important not to be angry or ashamed because you don't have what others have. That's pride, and pride often gets in the way of our ability to function on an even keel. Many children and young adults steal for that very reason, and that direction propels them into a life of crime. However, taking from others isn't a solution to any problem.

Not only is stealing against God's commandments, but it also shows a total disregard of someone else's hard work and efforts.

When a thief takes something from someone else, someone who has worked hard for that item, you not only let yourself down, but you let God down as well. God wants to help you, but you have to allow Him to do so. God will help you realize what is most important in life, if you only listen. Sometimes, the answers aren't what you expected.

Don't feel embarrassed if you have to rely on free lunch programs at school, or shopping at thrift stores, or need to apply for assistance with your local county or state government offices. Helping hands help us get through life, and sooner or later, we all need a helping hand. Remember that God's blessings come in many forms. Pride is a human emotion, one that God encourages us not to place too much emphasis in.

Yes, we rightly feel a sense of accomplishment when we achieve something or overcome a challenge, but it's also important to remember the phrase, "Pride goeth before the fall." Strive to be humble in all your dealings with people, and you will find that your attitudes, your behaviors, and your outlook on life are less stressful.

God Gives Us Purpose

When God provides us with a direction, He also gives us purpose. Sometimes, it's easy to wonder why we are where we are. Do we have a specific purpose in life? Are we to be a parent? On the other hand, are we supposed to achieve great things at work, at school, or in our social environment? Each of us wonders if we have a specific destiny to fulfill.

The bottom line is that we can all spend our lives wondering about our purpose, and never receive a clear or specific answer. Worrying about our purpose or destiny can be an exercise in futility unless you turn to God for guidance. There is no one on the face of the earth who knows what you should be doing - except God. If you listen carefully, and strive to follow the paths He lays before you, you will ultimately find the answer to those questions.

It is God who decides our purpose here on earth, and our life's plan. He created each and every one of us to fulfill a divine purpose, no matter how small or large that purpose is. The purpose that each of us fulfills its part of His eternal plan. It's extraordinarily reassuring to know that what we say, and that what we do, it ***does matter*** in the grand scheme of things. Our purpose, no matter whether we find it important and life changing or not, is essential.

You may never know the positive impact you may have on others. That impact alone may have a place in a chain of events in either your life or someone else's. Even the littlest things we do, say, or accomplish, during our lifetime are beneficial not only to ourselves, but to others. If you follow God's path, you will ultimately follow the destiny and purpose He has in store for you.

"The Lord will fulfill his purpose for me."
(Psalm 138:8)

As you say your prayers tonight, thank the Lord for providing everything you need and all that your heart desires, including acceptance, unconditional love, constant security, and a true purpose.

For many of us, not knowing exactly what we're supposed to do tomorrow, next week, or next year, can be frustrating. However, God's timing is perfect. For us, waiting for something to happen in our lives can be frustrating. All of us have to wait for something, whether it's learning how to drive,a phone call, a medical diagnosis, an event, a job, etc.

Waiting for an answer to our prayers is also extremely challenging. Many of us grow impatient and wonder if God is listening? If our prayers are not answered, what is preventing us from getting what we want? Sometimes, it seems like the more we want something, the more difficult it is to wait, and some of us even grow impatient with God. After all, if our prayers are answered, maybe God isn't really up there, or maybe, He doesn't feel as if you're good enough to offer you such a reward.

Don't fall into such thinking, as our desires for ourselves may not be the same as God's desires for us. God's timing is different than our own. Just because you want something today and don't receive it doesn't mean that you may not receive it in the future, in God's own good time. God sees things differently, from a different perspective. He not only knows what we want, but God also knows what is best for us in the grand scheme of our lives.

Remember that everything is part of God's divine order and will be done in His own time. Many of us forget this when we desire, hope, and pray for something.

"We know that all things work together for good for those who love God, who are called according to His purpose." (Romans 8:28)

Some of us deal with indecision and uncertainty in our lives, especially when we don't know what path to take. Some of us wait for financial security, while others wait for an addition to the family, a better marriage, or even a new job. Sometimes, it seems as if we spent our whole life waiting, for bigger and better things in our future. Regardless of what is happening today, there is always a chance that something better may happen tomorrow.

The Bible is filled with stories of people who "wait", and sometimes, that waiting can last weeks, months, years or even decades. Sometimes, waiting only lasts a few minutes. However, it's important to realize that it's not the length of time we wait, but how we handle that wait. The Scripture tells us that we should "wait on the Lord."

We must believe, with confidence and expectation, that God knows the direction we should take in our future. We are encouraged to trust that God will fulfill our "waiting", and in His good time.

Three steps will help you wait on the Lord, with patience, faith, knowledge and belief.

First - Trust in the Lord. If you doubt God's ability or willingness to hear as well as answer our prayers, we often feel discouraged and sometimes even begin to think that God has heard our prayers but is ignoring us. However, the Bible tells us that God is unchangeable, the same yesterday, today, and tomorrow, and that we can always rely on Him to provide the best possible direction or path for our lives.

Always remember that God said He will never leave or forsake us. If He doesn't answer your prayers right now, or you feel like you're being snubbed, remember that God may have another plan for you, and His timing is not your own. We must always trust in His plan.

Second - While we wait, we must strive to resist temptation. We must resist the urge to take matters into our own hands. Patience is a virtue, and extremely powerful. Practicing patience is very important in many circumstances and situations in our lives, and the Holy Spirit can fill you with patience when you feel as if you can't wait one minute longer. The safest place that we can find rest is within God's will. The stronger our faith and trust in God, the easier it will be to resist temptation.

Third - Pray. God is not deaf, and He does hear our prayers. Sometimes, your prayers will be answered and sometimes not, again depending on God's timing regarding those very prayers. During times of waiting, uncertainty, and indecision, it's not only important to keep on praying, but to pray the right way.

God hears us and will answer our prayers, but not always in the way we expect Him to. Sometimes, when we don't get the answers we want right away, we have a tendency to repeat that same prayer over and over again until we give up. It's important for us to give our requests or our needs to the Lord.

It's important to say thank you, in an attitude of expectancy. Always remember, that all our requests should be concluded with, "not my will, but yours, Lord." When we thank God in advance for answering our prayers, we're showing an active display of faith and demonstrating that we are confident in our expectations to God that we respect and believe in His awesome power to provide for us. Being in the *"will"* of God is the **safest place** we can ever be.

"Seek his will and he will direct your paths"
(Proverbs 3:6)

Here's a prayer to help you as you wait on God's perfect timing:

Dear Heavenly Father,

I have been waiting for _____so long now, and I come before You today to ask for Your help. I pray that You will increase my faith and patience so that I will put my whole trust in Your perfect timing and plan for my life. I will put my complete trust in You with confidence and eager expectation of Your answer, whatever the answer may be and whenever that answer may come.

Thank you for always being with me.
Thank you that You hear my prayers and will
answer in Your time and in Your way. You, Lord,
are without limits.
Thank you for Your unfailing word and that
You always keep Your promises to me. I believe
with my heart, mind, and soul Your plan for
my life is the best one possible, and I thank you
for Your answer.
Being in Your will is the safest place
I can ever reside.
In Jesus's name, Amen.

In such a way, we affirm God's perfect timing and our trust in God. Such affirmations also would knowledge His will and perfect order in revealing our direction or destination.

Creating Our Future

God can create the best future for you, if you follow His path. "For I know the plans I have for you, declares the Lord. Plans to prosper you and not to harm you, plans to give you hope and a future. Then you will call upon me, and I will listen to you. You will seek me and find me when you seek me with all your heart. I will be found by you, declares the Lord, and I will bring you back from captivity." (Jeremiah 29: 11–12)

Most of us like to plan out our days, and our lives. We chart a course that we think we should take, and set goals for all types of happiness and success along the way. Sometimes, we seek advice and guidance from friends, coworkers, and family members, hoping that they can help us make the right decisions when it comes to the direction or path we should follow in life. We also hope that these very same people want what's best for us, and yet, even those who love us may be torn in their loyalties or mistaken in their advice. After all, we're only human.

Sometimes, what someone else wants for you is not what you want for yourself or vice versa. However, if you put your faith in God and in God's guidance, you will find the direction that will make you happiest, and that is best for you.

God clearly promises us that He already has plans for us in place, and we only have to call upon Him to find out what those plans are in detail. Only God clearly sees our future and knows what is going to happen. No one else can guide you as confidently, honestly, and surely as God.

Remember that God will reveal His plan to you, but only if you're willing to ask and listen. This is not to say that we won't face difficult times, challenges or need to take detours in our life. Often, God gives us detours to get around or overcome to help us get to where we're going.

Isn't it wonderful that God clearly sees our future and can put us on the right path, knowing that no matter what happens along our journey, we'll end up at the best possible place for us, as God's children?

When you pray, ask the Lord to grant you the patience and wisdom to turn to Him for guidance. Let Him know that you trust in His desire to give you the best possible future and that you will slow down enough to listen to His guidance rather than to the rush to the world around you.

"Trust in him at all times..." (Psalm 62:8)

Chapter 8: Praying to God – The Coolest Conversations

Many people, from children to adults, feel self-conscious about praying. Some don't even want to admit they pray to God. For some reason, many people today believe that they should keep their beliefs hidden, in a closet, away from criticism, sarcasm, and in some cases, being made fun of.

This is especially true for kids, whether they're in elementary school, middle school, high school or college. However, don't let people make you think that being a Christian or that Christian living is uncool. It isn't. God loves you, and wants to have an intimate relationship with you. Don't be ashamed of admitting that you believe in God, trust in Him, and communicate with Him.

An Open Line of Communication to God

Some days, it's easy to feel like no one understands you, or no one believes in you, your capabilities, or in what you're trying to accomplish. However, isn't it nice to know that God always understands you? God always believes in you. We've mentioned it before and we'll say it again; God will never leave or forsake you. Remember that God planned your destiny before you were even born. You may not know what path to take ,or what direction your life will take you, but God does.

Your destiny is God's plan for your life. Every moment of every day, God understands what you're going through. God knows what you're feeling. You don't have to say it. He knows. God also knows how discouraged you can get at times, or disappointed, frustrated, or uncertain. He gives us a way out of such feelings. How? Trust in the Lord with all your heart and He will direct your paths. Lean on God, call out to Him, and He will answer you.

"Be strong and of good courage. Do not be afraid or dismayed." (1Chronicles 22:13)

Are You a Rebel?

Many people don't think of it this way, but did you know that Jesus was the original rebel? Not only was He a rebel, but He also had a cause. At the time of Jesus, and even among His own people, His village, and His neighbors and family, Jesus was considered a rebel; He stuck out like a sore thumb. He bucked tradition.

In many ways, He challenged the laws of the Old Testament in His effort to show the people the true meaning of those laws. Many people didn't understand Jesus and criticized Him, believing that He sought to destroy the laws of the Old Testament. This couldn't be further from the truth. However, like many today, and most especially teenagers, Jesus wasn't understood. In their minds, they truly believed He was "upsetting the apple cart."

Many of us admire people who do things that we are sometimes afraid to do ourselves. However, every time you take a stand for something you believe in, you are doing the same thing. When you stick up for what's right, or for what's fair, you may find that people either agree with you and support you or they disagree with you and criticize or condemn you.

The same happens when you stick up for God. Unfortunately, the truth is, you may be made fun of or criticized for your belief in something that no one can see, touch, or hear. However, for the true Christian, God is not invisible. If we listen carefully, we can hear Him. If we listen, He will show us the direction to take in life.

When good things happen to us, and we enjoy the benefits of life, we call ourselves lucky. However, luck has nothing to do with it. How many times have you been driving and seen an accident ahead of you? A mere minute sooner, and that might've been you. Or, what about that test you aced even though you were nervous about passing because you didn't study enough? Do you think it was just chance? It's not. In such times, believe that God is assisting you.

Many people doubt the existence of God because they don't know who He is. However, your life, and how you live it, can change those attitudes. In some cases, you and your belief in God may be the only glimpse of Him that others see. Through you, they may themselves develop a relationship with God and come into their own understanding with their faith. Because of this, it's important to let them know how much you believe and rely on God and need Him in your life.

You Can Believe that God is Cool

There's nothing quite as difficult as growing up as a teenager. From the years of 12 to 18 or even into our early 20s, our lives can literally feel like we're on a nonstop roller coaster ride. Sometimes, all we want to do is get off.

Sure, we experience highs, but we also experienced the lowest of lows. Sometimes we get so dizzy we don't know which way is up, or which way to turn. Our emotions are a mess, and when we feel low, we feel pretty darn lonely.

At the same time that our hormones are changing our bodies and our attitudes and emotions are all over the map, it's very difficult to find out who you're supposed to be. As if that isn't enough of a challenge, society, including our school friends, our peers, our parents and our teachers, put additional pressures on us. Our friends expect us to be cool, look cool, and act cool. It's especially important in our social school environment to make other people think we're cool as well.

However, do you believe that you are cool? It's important to believe that you are. Society and culture, especially in our middle and high school years, can be extremely challenging and frustrating. If we don't look just so, talk like this, or act like that, our friends and peers can be highly critical. Their comments, snickers and criticisms can slowly chip away at our self-esteem. However, at the same time, teachers, adults, and counselors are telling us that it's our responsibility to feel good about ourselves.

It's complicated, confusing, and extremely frustrating to maintain an even keel through these troublesome years. Many teenagers feel that Christianity, or believing in God isn't cool. Depending on where you live and the people you hang around with, you may have already experienced negative comments regarding God, belief in God, or Christian lifestyles. However, negative experiences with organized religion, whether at church, among youth groups, or at school is not the same as relating a negative experience with God on a personal level.

Think of it this way - religion might not always be cool, but God is. God is Cool. God is all about helping you become who you are. So why is God cool?

God is about *relationship* not religion. He wants you to develop a relationship with Him. He's your best friend. At some point, you've probably lost a friend, maybe even a best friend, or have had your heart broken by a friend. Many of us have experienced betrayal, or a friend talking about us behind our back, or a friend took something away from you, just because he or she knew you wanted it. However, God will never do anything like that. He loves you and wants what's best for you.

Friends come and go and relationships change, bloom, and, without warning, wither and die. However, God will never leave you. He promises to always be there for us. God has been there for you since the very beginning, and He will be there for you throughout eternity. Everyone wants someone they can count on through thick or thin, during our highs and our lows, during our joys and our grief. God is that someone.

In life, we often feel that we're misunderstood, or not understood at all. However, God is the only one who truly knows who you are, and you don't even have to explain it to Him! During your teenage years and youth, and even as you age, you change so fast you can hardly keep up with yourself. You don't even know who you are and your parents often wonder the same thing, and say so. Sometimes, it even seems as if our friends don't really care who we are. However, God knew you before you were even conceived. The Bible tells us that God has a plan for each and every one of us. God even knows how many hairs are on your head. Can your friends say that?

God knows your thoughts before you even think them. If you're tired of feeling lost or like nobody knows you, you know how exhausted, discouraging and depressing it can be. Nevertheless, you don't have to feel like that because God knows exactly who you are, who you can be, and who you want to be.

God knows what's best for you, even when you don't know or think otherwise. When everyone around you is demanding something from you, whether it's behavior, grades, what you should be wearing, or about a boyfriend, girlfriend or music, God cares only about you. All that extra stuff is just that - stuff.

The bottom line is that God is cool because He desires for you to be cool. Life is so much easier on you when you count on your best friend, and that best friend is God. Don't be afraid to talk to Him. He's always ready, willing, and able to listen.

God gives you your own identity. You don't have to worry about putting on a mask for others so that they'll see you in a certain way. God knows our true identity. He is the one that has made us whole and complete. He knows the most hidden parts of our hearts and souls. When we discover the power and presence of God within us, we have found our true identity. That identity doesn't depend on anyone else. We are, and always will be, unique creations of the master creator.

"I am God's child." (John 1:12)

Remember that the **mind** of God will always have the solutions to the problems you face in life. God will always be your cheerleader. Commit your life and your heart to God every day, and strive to live according to His will. Praise God throughout your day, and become absorbed in Him.

"If you abide in me, and my words abide in you, you will ask what you desire, and it shall be done for you." (John 15:7)

Conclusion: Stay on Track- With God You Can Face Anything in Life

It's not always easy to grow up in today's times, but stay on track. Acknowledge your respect for who God is and confess your sins. Strive to be a better person. Ask God for guidance, understanding in prayer, and live with an attitude of expectancy and faith. Trust that God can and does answer our prayers – but in His good time, and in His own wisdom.

Don't pray only when you're desperate or if you're afraid, or because nothing else has worked out. Pray from faith and in confidence, and with faith that God will fulfill your expectations in the best way possible for you, out of His own divine wisdom.

When you pray, pray in Jesus's name. When we pray in Jesus's name, we enter into a relationship with Jesus Christ, God's own son. In this way, we're able to take full advantage of His death on the cross as a payment for our sins by acknowledging His sacrifice in our prayers. It ties us to the new life of Christ's resurrection.

"Whatever you ask in my name, that I will do."
(John 14:13)

Every prayer is important, and every prayer counts. Our prayers exalt Him for who He is. Find the power of prayer. In His presence, we will find our greatest blessings.

Bottom line - walk in faith and in the knowledge that God is always there for you - every second, every minute, every hour. God will always be there for you when friends, family, peers and teachers fall away. God is the one who will always be there, yesterday, today, and tomorrow. His love for you will never change, but serve as a constant guide, supporter, comforter, and mentor in your life on Earth.

*"I can do all things through Christ
who strengthens me"* (Philippians 4:13)

It is cool to believe in God for love, acceptance, friendship, protection, and direction.

Be Inspired to Live for God ™ !

Special Prayer for You
Keep a Clear Mind

Dear Heavenly Father,

Thank You for Your amazing love.

Help me to be an example of Your love.

Take over every area of my life-my thoughts, my attitude

and my body.

Thank You for noticing me, loving me , calling me and using me

to bring glory to Your name.

I trust in You to guide and lead me.

In Jesus Name. Amen

About the Author

Robert Moment is a life coach, personal growth strategist, speaker and author of several life-transforming books.

Robert specializes in maximizing human potential for purpose, happiness and success. He is passionate about empowering individuals on how to experience God's love, peace, power, joy and prosperity (true spiritual wealth) in their lives.

With an ability to take the lessons he's learned in life and apply them to whatever situation someone else is in, Robert Moment excels in bringing out the best in people. His heart and love for people enables him to see who they were meant to be, and then, as a life coach and personal growth strategist, help them to implement a plan to help them reach their goals.

Robert Moment doesn't just think *out* of the box, *he throws the box away!* Pushing the envelope with innovative ideas that bring out the absolute best in people, his goal is to use his God-given skills to encourage and inspire others to find *and live* their life's purpose.

What can Robert Moment do for you? He can help you transform your adversities into life lessons that will spur you on to the life you are meant to have because he believes that behind every problem is an *opportunity for growth*. While you may not be able to discern what that is, Robert Moment will use his insight and wisdom to best determine what direction you should take.

With years of experience in the corporate sector working for Major Fortune 500 Companies such as Xerox, Sprint-Nextel, and CitiCorp, just to name a few, Robert Moment is now a highly sought-after life coach and personal growth strategist, with the ability to raise people up out of the muck and mire of confusion and doubt into the clear waters of endless possibilities! Robert specializes in maximizing human potential by bringing out the best in individuals to help them find their purpose and live a life of true happiness and success. He recognizes that even the most talented individuals often fail at achieving their goals because they have not yet grasped their life's purpose. Allow him a glimpse into your life and he will use his gifts to reveal to you how to change directions and head toward personal fulfillment and success.

Operate in the fullness of God's Plan for your life.

Because Robert Moment believes *everyone* on this earth *has* a purpose, his mission is to help people find it and *live it*. "Experience how good it feels to be happy in life and living your purpose." This is not just a slogan for Robert Moment – *it is a way of life*.

"Be Inspired to Live" ™ !

--- Robert Moment

Visit his website

www.AChristianYouth.com

Contact Robert for Speaking, Seminar and Workshop Opportunities

Email: *Robert@AChristianYouth.com*

More Information

This book is available for bulk sale. To inquire about pricing for twenty or more copies (sold at a substantial discount, non-returnable), please send an email message to:

Email: Robert@AChristianYouth.com

www.ingramcontent.com/pod-product-compliance
Lightning Source LLC
Chambersburg PA
CBHW071640050426
42443CB00026B/788